PET OWNER'S GUIDE TO THE
BULLMASTIFF

Janet Gunn

RINGPRESS

This book is dedicated to the members of the Southern Bullmastiff Society, whose barrage of queries during my term as Secretary prompted me to accumulate a much wider fund of knowledge than I might have acquired otherwise. I hope I have been able to provide answers on most topics.

ABOUT THE AUTHOR

Janet Gunn came from a family involved with the Bull Breeds for more than 40 years, initially Staffies, Boxers and Bulldogs. Prior to devoting herself full-time to Bullmastiffs, she owned and showed Great Danes, mainly in the 70s. Under the Flintstock affix, she and her husband, Alex, owned and bred numerous top-winning Bullmastiffs in the UK and abroad, the most notable being 1992 Crufts Best of Breed winner Ch. Lepsco Lady Elise of Flintstock (whose sire she owned). This bitch won the Challenge Certificate again at Crufts 1994. Formerly secretary of the Southern Bullmastiff Society, Janet has judged Bullmastiffs both in the UK and abroad.

ACKNOWLEDGEMENTS

My grateful acknowledgements to *Veterinary Notes for Dog Owners, ed Trevor Turner,* Bvet Med, MRCVS (Popular Dogs,1990); Di Williamson, for her valuable contribution on Behaviour; to Anne Lewis for information on the American show scene, and to the various handbooks and newsletters of the Bullmastiff Association, the British Bullmastiff League, the Northern Bullmastiff Club, the Southern Bullmastiff Society and the Welsh and West of England Bullmastiff Society, which collectively contain a wealth of information.

Cover photography: Blackslates Dream Chaser, owned by John and Muriel Bissat. Photo: Julia Barnes

Published by Ringpress Books,
A Division of INTERPET LTD,
Vincent Lane, Dorking, Surrey, RH4 3YX

Designed By Rob Benson

First published 2000
© Interpet Publishing. All rights reserved

ISBN 13   978 1 86054 187 2
ISBN 10   1 86054 179 9

Printed and bound in Hong Kong through Printworks International Ltd.

CONTENTS

INTRODUCING THE BULLMASTIFF 6

Early history (The gamekeeper's dog, Breed recognition); Characteristics (Guarding breed); Famous owners; The Bullmastiff outside Britain (American links, Australia and New Zealand, Europe).

THE BULLMASTIFF PUPPY 14

Finding a breeder; Assessing the litter; Deposit; Preparing for the new arrival (Security, Equipment, Documentation, Settling in, Other dogs, House-training); The first night.

CARING FOR YOUR BULLMASTIFF 24

Living accommodation; Crates; Outside kennel; Feeding your Bulmastiff; Grooming (Ears, Ticks and fleas, Teeth, Nails, Nose); Exercise; Development.

TRAINING AND SOCIALISING 34

Basic training (Sit, Stay, Recall, Lead-training, Heelwork; Training classes; The Bullmastiff in society; Problem solving; The role of play; Take it or leave it; Establishing hierarchy; Home alone.

5

IN THE SHOW RING   46

Ring training; Upholding standards;
Ring rapport; Showing in the UK
(Exemption show, Limit show,
Open show, Championship Show);
Showing in the USA; Jargon.

6

BREEDING BULLMASTIFFS   54

Selecting a stud dog; The mating;
Whelping the bitch; The birth;
Uterine inertia; Eclampsia; Mastitis;
Endoparasites.

7

HEALTH MATTERS   66

Anal glands; Bloat; Cancer; Cruciate
Ligament; Distichiasis; Entropion;
Eye infections in new-born puppies;
Fleas; Hip dysplasia; Hypertrophic
osteodystophy; Hyperthyroidism;
Mammary tumours; Mange;
Osteochondrosis; Panosteitis;
Persistent pupillary membrane;
Prostatic disease; Pyometra; Skin and
coat conditions; Vaginal hyperplasia;
Wet eczema; Worms.

1 Introducing The Bullmastiff

The Bullmastiff is a powerfully built dog of great strength. His temperament is reliable and faithful, though high-spirited and alert. When interested, the broad, deep head wrinkles expressively. These are big dogs, with the males weighing up to 60 kg (132 lbs), with bitches proportionally smaller, weighing around 50 kg (110 lbs). Because the breed was evolved as a working guard dog, capable of working rough terrain and holding his own against anything on four legs or two, some of the old working spirit is still there. Even though the Bullmastiff is a guarding breed, he can make a loyal and affectionate family pet, gentle and patient with children.

EARLY HISTORY

Although the exact origins of the Bullmastiff are open to conjecture, the breed as we know it today was bred for the sole purpose of accompanying and protecting the gamekeeper as he went about his task of apprehending poachers in mid-19th-century Britain.

THE GAMEKEEPER'S DOG

Before the name Bullmastiff was established, the gamekeeper's companion was variously called the 'Bull and Mastiff' and the 'Gamekeeper's Night Dog'. The requirement was for a dog of sufficient agility to pursue a man, together with the power to bring him to the ground and hold him there, without savaging. Numerous crosses were introduced over a period of time, including the St Bernard, Great Dane and the Bloodhound, before the combination of the Bulldog and the English Mastiff was established, with the ratio of 40 per cent Bulldog and 60 per cent Mastiff being preferred.

The Bulldog of the Victorian period was a considerably more

Brindle was the colour favoured by gamekeepers as it was less conspicuous at night.

The recognised colours for the Bullmastiff are fawn, red and brindle, with the brindle colouring favoured by gamekeepers in the early days, as being less conspicuous at night. Another requirement was that the dog should accompany his master silently and you will find to this day that the Bullmastiff rarely barks without good reason, which can be a distinct advantage for today's pet owner.

streamlined specimen than that which has been developed in recent years, and his agility, ferocity and tenacity, coupled with the weight and size of the Mastiff, made him a formidable poachers' opponent.

Some of the early Bullmastiffs were indeed terrors, but needed to be, as the penalty for poaching was death. Therefore any means of violence could be anticipated that might facilitate escape and capture. Hence the importance placed upon a dog with a broad, square skull with a good distance between the eyes, in the event that one eye might be put out by an assailant with a club or iron bar.

BREED RECOGNITION

As the breeding of these dogs became more prolific in the early part of the 20th century, the Kennel Club in Britain began registering the Bullmastiff as a Crossbreed and at that time the name was hyphenated: Bull-Mastiff. Most of the pedigrees contained both Bullmastiffs and Mastiffs, although the accuracy of some of the pedigrees is open to debate. However, it was not until 1924 that the Kennel Club officially registered the Bullmastiff as a separate breed. The first Breed Standard was drawn up in 1926 and subsequently revised in 1943, 1956, and then again in 1994. In 1928, Challenge Certificates were offered for the first time at Championship Shows.

Mr W. Burton, whose Bullmastiff, Thorneywood Terror, was exhibited extensively at gamekeepers' shows, kept a large kennel of Bullmastiffs. The Farcroft affix, belonging to Mr S.E. Moseley, can be traced back through almost every pedigree and his brindle bitch, Farcroft Silvo, was the first Bullmastiff ever to qualify for the title of Champion. Mr Toney's Roger of the Fens became a well-known Champion and his name is also to be found behind most modern Bullmastiff strains.

A well-socialised Bullmastiff accepts children and shows a special gentleness with them.

The popularity of the breed has waxed and waned over the years; it is perhaps surprising to learn that, in the 1920s and 1930s, entries in excess of 70 exhibits were not uncommon at shows. Although twice that figure is anticipated today at a Championship Show in Britain, the number of litters bred and registered annually with the Kennel Club has multiplied disproportionately. There was a proliferation of regional breed clubs during the pre-war years and they still flourish today.

CHARACTERISTICS
Although the modern Bullmastiff will instinctively guard should the need arise, careful breeding has modified the more extreme protective characteristics so that his present-day role is more generally regarded as that of a family pet, which suits his nature very well. Although normally gentle and patient with children and amenable to allcomers, it must be stressed that constant socialisation is essential in the young, growing puppy while the long-term character of the dog is forming.

A GUARDING BREED
As with most guarding breeds, a Bullmastiff, if left alone for long periods when young, can become

overprotective towards his home and owners, and once antisocial behaviour is established, it is difficult to correct.

The Bullmastiff has a unique character and, although the individual temperaments may differ vastly from one another, there is, underlying each one, the basic loyal, affectionate and protective nature that has endeared the breed to a growing number of devotees over the years. A Bullmastiff's devotion to his owner is legendary and a more loyal and affectionate companion would be hard to find. This by no means makes him a 'one-man-dog', as his affection and trust is best enjoyed as a family member whose loyalty embraces all those in the household.

Nonetheless, although his original guarding instincts have been greatly domesticated, he should always be treated with respect, as he has an intelligent and sometimes surprisingly sensitive nature that should not be abused by indifferent handling, particularly in his formative months. Rough or insensitive treatment can result in either aggression or timidity and, although it is most uncommon to find a Bullmastiff who will challenge his owner, his behaviour towards others is dictated by his early experiences.

An increasing number of Bullmastiffs are being used as therapy dogs, visiting those who are in hospitals or nursing homes and others who are no longer in a position to own a dog of their own, where his calm and steady temperament comes into its own. However, when action is called

This is a breed that must always be treated with respect.

for, he can be surprisingly fast. You should have no illusions about his speed and agility if put to the test! He has great strength and, for this reason, it is not recommended that young children be left in charge of, or allowed to exercise, a Bullmastiff unaccompanied by an adult. In fact, an undisciplined male would be difficult for a good many adults to control if the necessity arose.

FAMOUS OWNERS

A number of celebrities and public figures made the Bullmastiff their choice. Lord Londonderry was a great enthusiast and successfully promoted the breed in the show ring in the early 1930s, as did HRH the Duke of Gloucester.

In 1936, the Arsenal football team chose a Bullmastiff as their mascot, aptly naming him 'Gunner'; and the Hollywood film sets of the 1930s saw a Bullmastiff in the company of Douglas Fairbanks Snr. It is reported that President Roosevelt owned a Bullmastiff during the Second World War, although efforts to trace a photograph of the pair have proved fruitless.

Champion jockey Sir Gordon Richards was such a devotee of the breed that he donated a trophy to the Southern Bullmastiff Society, which is still awarded to this day.

In recent years, the blockbuster series of 'Rocky' films featured a Bullmastiff personally owned by the star of the films, Sylvester Stallone.

THE BULLMASTIFF OUTSIDE BRITAIN

The first Bullmastiffs to be exported from England went from the Farcroft kennel to the United States in 1930. All of these early Kennel Club licensed exports went to the United States. Canada followed suit in 1945. However, in the 1930s, Bullmastiffs were being exported, without licences, to South Africa where they were used to guard the diamond mines.

AMERICAN LINKS

The Bullmastiff became increasingly popular in the US, achieving recognition by the American Kennel Club in 1933. John D. Rockefeller imported Bullmastiffs in the 1930s as gamekeepers' dogs to guard his Pocantico estate in New York. The Pocantico affix was subsequently registered with the American Kennel Club.

Bullmastiffs are now popular worldwide.

breeds in California under the Bullmast affix.

Each year, the American Bullmastiff Association holds a 'Specialty' (the equivalent of a breed Championship Show in England) in a different part of the United States. This attracts huge numbers of Bullmastiffs, breeders and fanciers from all over the world.

Although Bullmastiffs are regularly exported to the US, importation into England is rare – due, to some extent no doubt, to the English quarantine laws.

AUSTRALIA AND NEW ZEALAND

The Bullmastiff has enjoyed popularity in Australia and New Zealand since the 1940s, with Australian breeders first establishing their major breeding programmes with imports from the Bulmas kennel during the 1950s. Since then, imports have been secured from most of the significant English breeding kennels.

In the 1940s, renowned English breeder, Cyril Leeke of the Bulmas affix, exported his stock to Leonard Smith in the US and his daughter, Patricia O'Brien, still

Many New Zealand bloodlines emanate from Australian stock and therefore indirectly from England, although a number of breeders have also imported directly from British kennels.

EUROPE

The exchange of breeding stock between England and mainland Europe is more commonplace and will probably develop still further in the future with the lifting of British quarantine restrictions currently under review.

Bullmastiffs have become increasingly popular in the Scandinavian countries, with original breeding stock from England. The Bulmas kennels exported to Finland in the 1950s and numbers have progressively increased, with many English Bullmastiff fanciers attending breed club shows in different parts of Finland as spectators and judges.

Numbers in Sweden are fewer but, as with Finland, the original

The impressive physique makes an eye-catching sight in the show ring.

stock hailed from England and current breeding stock is combined with bloodlines from Finland, Norway and Denmark.

Although Bullmastiffs have been bred in Germany since just after the Second World War, it is only fairly recently that their popularity has increased, with the exchange of exports between English and German kennels. This is perhaps not surprising, in view of the number of German breeds which have enjoyed such universal popularity over many years. However, more and more Bullmastiffs are being introduced to the European show scene with great success and are subsequently being accepted as a welcome alternative to the native breeds.

In France, Spain, Portugal and Italy, the Molosser breeds have historically been recognised since the early days of dog fighting. Following the abolition of these cruel sports, their numbers decreased, although there has been a strong regenerative surge of interest in all of these breeds over the past decade.

In France, the Bullmastiff has always retained his popularity since his introduction in the 1950s, although his cousin, the Dogue de Bordeaux, is widely considered the most popular of the Molosser breeds in his native country.

In Spain, popularity of the breed declined until the early 1980s, when breeding stock was imported from England. Since then there has been increased interest in breeding, with the importation of stock from Scandinavia and the United States.

Bullmastiff popularity has progressively increased in Belgium, with breeders importing strains from England and using German stock to expand their bloodlines.

Very recently, great interest has also been shown by Eastern bloc countries, with exports to Russia, Latvia and Estonia.

Many of the Molosser breeds, historically linked with dog fighting and a ferocious guarding instinct, have been penalised by non-registration and muzzling in public places. The Bullmastiff, however, due to his stable temperament and ability to combine a natural guarding instinct with a gentle, affectionate nature is spared these restrictions and restraints.

2 The Bullmastiff Puppy

Before embarking upon the all-important decision to own a Bullmastiff, you must make sure that everyone in the household finds the idea acceptable. What appears at eight weeks of age to be a lovable, cuddly, playful baby, will grow into a powerful, sometimes wilful adult, who will need firm handling.

This is not a dog that the kids can take for a run in the park, or that can be left alone to his own devices for long periods. We are talking about a large, intelligent, thinking dog, who will try every trick in the book to exert his personality over yours to get his own way. This, of course, is part of the charm of a Bullmastiff.

If you are too lenient with a mischievous pup, because he is so amusing and appealing, he can quickly take charge of a household and be ruling the roost before you know it! Not in an unpleasant way, you understand, just because

the Bullmastiff tends to think he is human, and what is good enough for you is good enough for him: same sofa, same armchair, same bed.

Now, if you are prepared for this and are perfectly happy to live that way – his way – then you will have the next best (or better) thing to a human companion. However, if you would prefer to live life on your own terms, you must be prepared to spend some time teaching him who is the boss. This is a much happier state of affairs for him, as he will feel secure in the knowledge that he has a pack leader.

FINDING A BREEDER

Having accepted this, and still ready for the challenge, you must choose your Bullmastiff puppy sensibly. Contact your national Kennel Club and ask for the telephone number of the secretary of your regional Bullmastiff

Bullmastiff puppies are most appealing, but you must consider the size and strength of an adult dog.

Society; seek their advice and set about seeing as many Bullmastiffs as you can.

The best and quickest way is to attend a breed show where there are possibly a hundred or more present. Take the family, and have a good look at the different types in and around the show ring.

Decide whether you want a dog or a bitch, bearing in mind that the male Bullmastiff is less easy to cope with than the female, being physically more powerful and instinctively more assertive.

Ask the club secretary if there is a litter available that could be recommended. Contact the breeder and make an appointment to visit, but not until the pups are at least four to five weeks old. To the untrained eye, there is really nothing to distinguish them until then.

ASSESSING THE LITTER
Whether you are looking for a Bullmastiff to show or purely as a pet, make sure that the whole litter looks healthy, happy and in good condition.

During the course of your visit, it is inevitable that the pups will do what they do best: make a mess! Do not avert your gaze – make sure that the motions are nicely formed. A puppy with watery motions may be harbouring an infection and it is easy for a puppy to dehydrate and become ill very quickly at this age. Do not take a sickly puppy because you feel sorry for him; there is enough heartache in owning dogs without seeking it out.

Do not be misled by a breeder calling a puppy 'show quality'. At eight weeks of age, there are no

guarantees that a Bullmastiff will mature into a show specimen, however promising he may look in the nest. Most ethical breeders will sell you a nicely made, healthy pup as a pet, and if he does well in the show ring, then it is a bonus.

There should be no difference in price between a male and female puppy. The only difference in the price of a puppy should be where there is an obvious fault – a badly cranked tail, for example.

The term 'crank' is used to describe a short tail which is malformed to varying degrees, sometimes badly twisted with the vertebrae fused together giving a knotted appearance. This is a throwback from the Bulldog and, although it will exclude the Bullmastiff from the show ring, it will not affect the animal in any other way.

A puppy with a 'crank' tail (front) is not suitable for showing, but is perfectly acceptable as a pet.

A black muzzle is often favoured in the show ring.

Look for a puppy with a nice black muzzle; this is always more attractive if you want to show. But, here again, if the pigment is not very dense, as long as he is a healthy, sturdy Bullmastiff, this is not a major fault.

Obviously, the dam will be in residence, although not necessarily still with the puppies. An eight-week-old litter has sharp teeth and toenails which can be very uncomfortable hanging on to mother. Often, an outside stud dog is used, so it is quite normal and acceptable that the sire will not always be present.

DEPOSIT
Do not part with a deposit until you have selected your puppy. If a breeder asks for a deposit prior to your seeing the litter, find another breeder. It is not unknown for the less ethical breeder to demand a deposit before a litter is even born! Be warned, this is not acceptable practice and such obviously mercenary tactics should be actively discouraged.

PREPARING FOR THE NEW ARRIVAL
Having made your choice, make sure that your home is prepared in advance for the new arrival.

SECURITY

The first priority is a completely secure garden. If there is a gap in the fencing, you can be sure that your puppy will find it. Never take a chance by temporarily blocking up a possible escape hatch because your Bullmastiff will have no trouble in finding a way round it. If there are weak spots in your fencing, it is better to erect some chain-link to enclose the entire perimeter rather than risk a lost puppy.

Puppies are great explorers, so make sure your garden is safe and secure.

EQUIPMENT

Decide where your puppy's bed will be and furnish it with chews and toys so that it will be a happy and comfortable place for him to retire to.

You will need two stainless steel bowls for food and water; do not waste time with either plastic (chewed within minutes) or porcelain (easily broken). Make sure you have a supply of his regular food: the breeder will advise you of his needs.

DOCUMENTATION

The accepted age for a puppy to leave the nest is eight weeks. If a breeder assures you that it is normal for the puppy to be collected at six weeks of age, either insist on waiting until the pup is eight weeks of age or find another breeder.

When you collect your puppy, the breeder should provide you with a four- or five-generation pedigree, a registration certificate to your national Kennel Club (or, failing this, a letter confirming application of registration and guaranteeing that the document will be forwarded once issued by the Kennel Club), diet sheet, worming certificate, insurance cover note and possibly a vaccination certificate against parvovirus (not every breeder has this inoculation given prior to departure, but some like to provide this additional safeguard).

SETTLING IN

It is comforting for the puppy if the breeder can provide a piece of blanket with a familiar smell to accompany him into his new

Introduce the family, but make sure the pup is not overwhelmed by too much attention.

surroundings; you can place it in his bed on arrival.

If you have a young family, try not to let them overwhelm the puppy as soon as he arrives. First, let him have a good sniff round the area where his bed is located.

OTHER DOGS

Great care must be taken when introducing a new canine addition into the home where a Bullmastiff is already 'in residence'.

The appearance of a puppy is generally well tolerated as he poses

Give the puppy a chance to explore his new home.

no threat to the established Bullmastiff at such an early age, but it is not recommended to take on two male Bullmastiffs in the same household.

The happiest combination of living partners is, naturally, a male and female, who will spend their lives devoted to one another. The obvious problem of the bitch's season can be overcome by spaying, which can take place between the first and second heat.

Two bitches will generally live in harmony together but care should be taken when one is on heat, as a hormone imbalance could affect the temperament of a normally good-natured bitch.

A young puppy of either sex should never be left unsupervised with a mature dog, as injury can easily occur to the young one purely through rough play with the heavier animal. Additionally, care should be taken not to leave toys around when discarded, as a fight could ensue if one dog takes the other's favourite plaything. Bones should never be given to unsupervised dogs either. Do not leave toys around with children in the house, as a perfectly innocent accident can happen if a dog tries to snatch a toy in play.

Possessiveness over the food

A male and a female Bullmastiff will often live together in harmony, but introductions must be carefully supervised.

bowl is not unusual but I have found, when keeping two puppies of a similar age, that it keeps their natures sweet if they continue to share a large puppy tray of food into adulthood. I have two seven-year-old litter sisters who were reared in this manner and still share their food bowl with each other; this does not mean that they would share it with any other dog!

Extreme caution must be exercised should a visitor wish to bring a mature dog into your home. Only the most placid Bullmastiff would take kindly to a strange canine invading his territory, and it is not fair to expect him to do so.

HOUSE-TRAINING

Have plenty of newspapers in stock as a house-training aid. It is unlikely that your Bullmastiff will be house-trained before he arrives, so newspaper on the kitchen floor near to the door will let him know where to go. Most litters are raised on newspaper alongside their sleeping area, so your puppy will be familiar with this.

It is quite likely that he will need to relieve himself after the journey, so make sure that the newspapers are in place and, once he has recognised that this is his toilet area, he should have no trouble returning to it.

Within a few days, if you place

Vigilance is the key to house-training.

the papers by the outside door, you will be able to see when he needs to perform his toilet and can place him outside. If you follow a routine of placing the puppy in the garden when he first wakes and after each meal, you will soon have him house-trained.

Without doubt, a summer puppy is easier to train, as both he and you will be happy to stay outside for as long as it takes if the weather is dry and warm.

Be patient if there are some accidents while he is still young. Do not be harsh with a puppy if he is not so quick to learn; we

would not scold a baby for wetting its nappy, would we?

THE FIRST NIGHT

It is unlikely that the breeder will have fed your Bullmastiff before he embarks on the journey to his new home, so have something tempting for him to eat after he has familiarised himself with his surroundings.

Coping with a lonely puppy on his first night away from littermates is not an easy task. It could well be that your pup will settle contentedly into his bed and not murmur until morning, as Bullmastiffs are extremely adaptable. However, there is the possibility that he will be unsettled and will protest loudly.

For the first few nights, I think it is kinder to be sympathetic and make sure that you are close at hand so that he can sense your presence. If he persists with his complaints when left on his own, you must harden your heart and ignore his protests until he learns that you will not always come when he calls. A radio playing softly in his room may comfort him.

Your puppy will miss his littermates to begin with.

3 Caring For Your Bullmastiff

The most important thing to remember when rearing a Bullmastiff puppy is that care and caution will result in a strong, sound adult.

LIVING ACCOMMODATION
Whether your dog is living in the house or in a kennel, his quarters must be clean, warm, dry and as free from draughts as possible.

For a dog living in the house, a large plastic bed is popular and easy to keep clean, coupled with a good-quality washable rug that can be machine-washed and dried quickly.

CRATES
I think if you were to ask any breeder which is the most invaluable canine item ever

It is important to establish 'house rules' at an early stage.

A crate should be regarded as a safe haven for your puppy.

invented as a training aid or device, most would reply "the crate"! This eighth wonder of the world has salvaged the sanity of many a household and is undoubtedly the kindest and most comfortable way of keeping a puppy out of mischief until he is old enough to know better.

The most practical and versatile crate for use by the pet owner is the collapsible wire mesh variety with a removable plastic or wooden base for easy cleaning, and a piece of washable fleecy rug inside to ensure a comfortable den. This type of crate can be used in the home or in the car and is easily transported, so that your dog has his 'mobile home' wherever he may travel.

If your Bullmastiff puppy is introduced to a crate when he is first brought home, he will regard it as his own secure haven, to which he can retreat whenever he feels the need, either to rest or to take a favourite chew or toy. The owner has the benefit of complete peace of mind when leaving the puppy alone for short periods, safe in the knowledge that he is not harming himself or getting into bad habits, such as chewing a handy piece of furniture or eating a poisonous pot plant. Remember that any puppy will chew if left unsupervised; it is up to the owner to remove the temptation!

When purchasing a crate, regard it as a long-term investment. There is no point in buying one to fit a puppy that will outgrow it in a few months. A minimum size should be 27 ins high x 24 ins wide x 30 ins long, which will enable him to stand up and turn around comfortably. This will also fit the average estate car. Ideally, a custom-built crate for the car and a separate, larger one for the home is most practical.

The location of the crate in the home is important, as it should not be regarded as a place of isolation. A corner of either the living room or the kitchen, free from draughts, and where most family activities take place, is best. Always ensure that there is a piece of good-quality washable rug to fit the crate at all times so that your dog does not acquire calluses on his hocks and elbows due to these pressure points contacting a hard surface. A small water bowl and holder can also be hooked on to the mesh inside the crate for those times when the gate has to be closed.

OUTSIDE KENNEL
If your Bullmastiff is living outside, the kennel should be soundly constructed of wood or concrete with either a stable-type door or a hatch that may be raised or lowered by means of a weight. An attached run should be at least 10 ft long by 4 ft wide. As my kennels are equipped with heating and light, I find it cleaner to use a raised bench area with a plastic bed on top.

Each bed is furnished with a piece of washable rug, but this is governed entirely by whether the inhabitant of the kennel is content to use it as bedding or whether he perceives it as a temporary plaything, which he feels compelled to shred within minutes of its arrival! A variety of bedding materials are available.

Other options include shredded paper (regarded by some as a delicacy), wood shavings (ditto), or straw, which is warm and keeps the dogs sweet-smelling, but which you must have the means to dispose of on a regular basis.

The base for the entire kennel area should be concreted, gently sloping to allow for efficient drainage. A power hose is useful to maintain proper hygiene and the runs should be washed down with an appropriate disinfectant every day. Stale faeces are a source of bacteria, also encouraging flies and rodents, and should never be allowed to accumulate.

Feeding bowls should be raised to shoulder level; either freestanding or fixed, but I prefer the type which hook or bolt on to the run panels for the kennels.

FEEDING YOUR BULLMASTIFF
Each breeder has his own method of feeding and, therefore, the new Bullmastiff owner should receive a diet sheet upon collection of the puppy. However, the following is a guide to my preferred feeding regime and forms part of the information sheet I give to all new owners.

The Bullmastiff is a fast-growing breed so it is essential to provide top-quality nutrition.

From eight weeks to three months, four meals a day, comprising:

Breakfast:
One large cup of good-quality complete puppy food (either soaked or dry, depending on the puppy's preference) with one scrambled, boiled or fried egg and a pint of milk. Raw eggs should never be given, particularly egg white.

Lunch:
Half a pound (198g) of raw minced (chopped) beef (20 per cent fat content but *not* pet mince), or cooked, boneless white meat. Beef, lamb or heart may be fed raw, but chicken, fish or rabbit should be cooked and boneless.

Dinner:
The same as breakfast but without egg and milk. Some tinned puppy food may be mixed in if the puppy needs some tempting.

Supper:
A tin of rice pudding and a rusk to chew on at bedtime usually ensures a peaceful night.

From three months to six months you will probably find that the puppy weans himself off the milky feed at night.

Digestion will be greatly aided if food bowls are raised to shoulder height.

From six months to a year, you will normally find that he will only take two meals a day, which should comprise:

Breakfast:
A good-quality 'junior' complete food, the amount to be increased in proportion to age and size of the puppy.

Dinner:
1-2lbs (0.454kg-0.907kg) of a meat feed.

It is better to feed two good-quality meals than rely on bulk to fill him up. It is infinitely safer to feed twice a day, rather than overload a hungry dog's stomach (see Chapter Seven: Bloat).

Each Bullmastiff puppy varies in his requirements, although common sense hopefully prevails. If in any doubt at all, do consult the breeder of your puppy who should be willing and able to advise you.

Do not expect your Bullmastiff puppy to prosper on a diet of ordinary canned dog food and mixer biscuit, however palatable this may be. Any dog that matures into a strapping ten-stone specimen needs specialised nutrition to ensure that his bones grow healthily to support his heavy physique.

Food and water bowls should be raised to shoulder level; bowl holders for this purpose are available at most good pet stores.

As your dog matures, his feeding requirements change, and it is important to reduce the level of protein in his diet.
In the elderly Bullmastiff, a complete food should contain only a maximum of 16 per cent protein. As with humans, the elderly dog tends to put on weight, and this should be sensibly monitored.

Unfortunately, the lifespan of a Bullmastiff is only expected to be around ten years, although the occasional veteran has been known to survive for several more. However, he is far more likely to stay healthy and reach a good old age if he is kept fit and active throughout his life.

GROOMING

The Bullmastiff is easily maintained and needs little more than a daily brush with a grooming glove which removes any dead hair. As with most short-haired dogs, they tend to shed

Accustom your puppy to being groomed and then he will learn to accept the routine.

their coat throughout the year and therefore it is essential that this minimal requirement is adhered to unless you want your clothes and carpet to constantly bear witness to their presence.

Kennel dogs will shed their coats more drastically as the elements dictate, and a stripping comb is recommended to clear out any woolly areas.

EARS

Careful attention should be paid to the ears to make sure they are kept clean and free from wax. Your veterinarian should be consulted whenever you notice your dog shaking his head and carrying one ear lower than the other one, if his behaviour is not remedied by your usual cleansing routine. Many Bullmastiffs have a narrow ear canal and it is not uncommon for a build-up of wax to occur.

Regular cleansing and, if necessary, the application of drops to break down the blockage should maintain good health. In the summer months, it is easy for a grass seed to become embedded in the ear canal and this needs professional treatment. Similarly, a nasal infection can be instigated by a grass seed being inhaled and causing a small blockage.

The Bullmastiff will shed his coat once a year.

TICKS AND FLEAS

These can be a problem in the summer months when your Bullmastiff is more likely to come into contact with long grass or to run where sheep and cattle have been grazing.

Fleas are not as visibly easy to detect but a tick will soon make its presence felt. Always run your hands over your dog following walks in the countryside – once a tick has burrowed into the skin, it can be difficult to remove cleanly.

All sorts of home remedies have been suggested over the years but the application of one of the modern specific deterrents available, either from your vet or from a good pet store, is probably the most successful treatment.

Once the tick has released its grip, it should be plucked out carefully with tweezers, making sure that the head of the parasite has been completely removed. An antispetic solution should then be applied to the spot.

TEETH

A regular check should be kept on teeth and gums. If a teeth-cleaning routine is followed while your dog is still a youngster, it will prevent plaque building up on the teeth, which can lead to gum infections and troublesome teeth in later life. It will also keep your dog's breath sweet.

NAILS

Nails should be short. If left unattended, long nails will cause pain and the feet to splay. There are several types of nail-clipper on the market, but a young pup's sharp nails can be dealt with by small nail scissors. As he grows, either the guillotine or heavy-duty clipper will be needed.

Guillotine clippers should be used when trimming an adult's nails.

Never allow your dog's toenails to grow so long that the quick is damaged when clipping. This is painful for the dog and will only result in a real struggle every time the clippers appear. With regular trimming, followed by a treat and plenty of praise on completion, your dog will accept this as part of his grooming routine.

NOSE

A regular application of Vaseline (pharmacy-grade petroleum jelly) on your dog's nose will guard against it becoming dry and cracked. The appearance of an otherwise handsome specimen is so often marred by the neglect of a regular grooming routine.

EXERCISE

The Bullmastiff is a large, heavy dog, and has a great deal of growing to pack into the first 18 months of his life. For this reason, forced exercise should not be undertaken until the bones and joints have formed sufficiently to withstand actual 'walks'. A romp in the garden is sufficient for a newly acquired puppy until he is six months of age. Short walks of about ten minutes' duration can then be given to accustom him to the lead and to teach him road sense, gradually progressing to longer walks as the limbs strengthen.

Prolonged walking should not be undertaken until around 18 months of age. Free running in a large area, such as a field, should be avoided while your Bullmastiff is still growing. Do not be tempted to overexert a youngster too soon just because both you and he would find it enjoyable – it really is not worth the risk of a permanently lame dog.

Care should also be taken in the house to prevent a puppy from climbing stairs. Should such an eventuality occur, *do not* call him down. Go up and carry him down. Immeasurable damage can be inflicted on the shoulder joints

Restrict exercise to short sessions during the vulnerable growing period.

in such a situation. A stair-gate is a useful investment for the puppy's health and your own peace of mind.

Similarly, no jumping from the back of a car must be allowed until your dog is mature enough to handle it. Ease him out with one hand on his collar and the other under his chest.

Although capable of sustained exercise when mature, the Bullmastiff is not demanding and will be happy to take as much or as little exercise as you are able to give him, which makes him a comfortable companion to live with.

To allow your Bullmastiff off the lead in a public park or on common land where there are other dogs loose is a risk not worth taking; there is always the danger of a fight with another dog which brings the breed into disrepute. Inevitably, the large dog is always condemned, whether condemnation is justified or not.

DEVELOPMENT

Do not be alarmed if, at around five or six months of age, your Bullmastiff appears to have inherited the physical characteristics of a Great Dane! It is quite normal for the fast-growing puppy to go through a very 'leggy' stage, accompanied by ears flying in every direction while teething. Do not despair. By the time he reaches 12 months, you will be able to recognise the typical features re-emerging, which were evident in the baby you acquired at eight weeks of age.

Development from 12 months onwards is rapid. Both head and body broaden and mature, although full maturity is not expected before three years of age.

The adult Bullmastiff will adapt to the amount of exercise you are able to give him.

4 Training And Socialising

Early training and socialisation are essential, as an unruly or aggressive Bullmastiff is no pleasure to own. Inevitably, the first command to be put into operation is the word "No", which should be delivered in a firm tone of voice, and the youngest puppy very soon understands when he is doing something wrong.

The next most important word, to me, is "Wait". Make sure your Bullmastiff 'waits' to let you go through a door ahead of him and 'waits' for his food until you are ready to give it to him. This is basic training to teach your dog that you are in control of him and not the other way round.

If your dog starts pushing through doors ahead of you, refuses to vacate your chair and is allowed to win a tug-of-war with a toy, it is simply his way of imposing his will over yours. This can easily be avoided if simple procedures are put into operation right from the start.

BASIC TRAINING
All training, however basic, requires a great deal of patience, so do not scold your puppy if he takes a little time to learn. You will be rewarded in the end by owning an obedient and well-behaved puppy, a fact which will stand him in good stead for the rest of his life.

It is unlikely that your puppy will have been named before you collect him, and the first thing you must do is to familiarise him with your chosen name, as this will precede any basic training command you will give him. For example, say "Bruno" – then wait a second or two to ensure that you have his attention – then give the command, such as "Sit", "Stay" or "Come". Always keep your puppy on your left-hand side, from which you will commence every obedience exercise.

Basic commands, such as "Sit", "Stay", and "Down" are easily taught at a very early age and the Bullmastiff is intelligent and willing to please his master. Put aside a short period of time each day for training. Short regular periods of training are most productive, as they will not overtax the puppy's attention span. All training should be regarded as fun, with enthusiastic praise and rewards for each command carried out successfully.

SIT

For the command "Sit", it is best to kneel next to your puppy,

keeping him on your left side. Place your left hand on his bottom and your right hand on his chest, then push both hands together while using his name and the command: "Sit". You will find that the puppy soon responds to the command, after which you will progress to one simple hand movement above the puppy's eyes when giving the command, and eventually to no physical signals at all.

STAY

Once your puppy is obeying your "Sit" command, progress to the "Stay" exercise. With your puppy sitting on your left, and you holding his lead in your right hand, give the command "Bruno, Stay", while making a left hand signal directly in front of his nose with the palm towards him. The fact that you are standing in front of him will block any forward movement he may try to make. Stay in this position for a short time and slowly remove your hand from in front of his nose. Then return to your original position on his right side and, kneeling, praise him thoroughly for his efforts.

The Bullmastiff must learn to accept his subordinate role in your family 'pack'.

TRAINING EXERCISES

Start training as soon as your Bullmastiff arrives home. This pup is learning to wait, and then to respond to the command "Come".

After a few days of this initial training, take a step back from your puppy after you have turned to face him, with his lead held loosely. You should soon have him sitting confidently enough to increase the number of steps until you can back away as far as the lead will allow. Stand in this position for a short time.

You eventually progress to the point when he does not move at all when you are backing away from him. You can then try laying the lead on the floor, or removing it altogether. By the time you have reached this stage, your Bullmastiff pup should stay without you turning in front of him. You can then simply give the command, "Bruno, Stay" and walk directly away from him.

RECALL
Once you have mastered the Sit-Stay training, you can progress to the Come exercise. For this, follow the Stay routine with him on the lead. Walk to the end of the lead, turn to face him and, after a few moments, give the command "Bruno, Come". Make this command a very happy one, and, if he seems unsure, because of his Stay training, gently encourage him, bringing him forward on the lead and turning with him until he is on your right-hand side. You can then guide him back to your left-hand side from whence all exercise commences. Let him sit there for a while and then praise him profusely.

LEAD-TRAINING
Prior to lead-training, introduce your Bullmastiff puppy to a braid collar that you can leave on him, so he gets used to the feel of it around his neck. Attaching a loose lead and slowly walking alongside him should not then prove too much of an ordeal.

Should your dog be off the lead, it is absolutely essential that he will return to you when called. We have all witnessed a mischievous dog getting within a hair's-breadth of his owner and then darting off, enjoying the antics of his owner trying to capture him, and there is nothing more frustrating or time-wasting than being caught in this situation.

However tempting it may be, never chastise your Bullmastiff once you have him in your grasp, however long it may have taken to get him there. Praise him and make a fuss of him, give a tidbit; soon he will learn that coming when he is called is more fun than running away. A little patience will result in an ultimately happier relationship for both you and your dog.

Lead-training is probably the most important exercise to teach when you are working with a large, powerful breed.

HEELWORK

Training your pup to walk to Heel is fairly simple once the Sit-Stay exercises have been accomplished. Begin by having your pup sit on your left-hand side, on his lead, and – after getting his attention by calling his name – give the command "Heel" and walk briskly forward, always with your left foot first. Walk as fast as you can, keeping him close to your left side with his shoulders more or less level with your left knee; this way, he will not be able to cross over in front of you. Go forward, making right turns, left turns and about-turns, all the time praising him and encouraging him. If he makes a mistake, say "No" and show him what you want him to do.

TRAINING CLASSES

Most areas have classes for Obedience or Ring Training and either of these are suitable for socialising puppies with dogs of all ages and types, and will also teach him to accept being handled by different people.

As soon as it is safe to do so, following his initial inoculations, it is important that a puppy is gently introduced to the noise and activity of everyday life: traffic,

Despite all the care you take with training, problems can still occur.

crowds of people, children, etc. If acclimatised to these from an early age, the puppy will react in a stable manner and will soon accept any situation that he encounters. A puppy that lives a sheltered or isolated existence can easily become shy, or aggressive through fear, when confronted with sights and sounds which are unfamiliar to him, and this can lead to permanent behavioural problems.

THE BULLMASTIFF IN SOCIETY

We live in a society where antisocial dogs are a problem, not only to their owners and all who come into contact with them, but also to themselves.

The one most likely to pay the highest price, as the result of an incident of any kind, is the dog – he very often has to pay with his life.

None of us want this to happen and we all want to protect our dogs but, frequently, we actually cause the problem in the first place. How? By unwittingly teaching the dog that he has the right to challenge humans and, if necessary, use whatever means he has at his disposal to control them or to test their strength. At the end of the day, this can mean using his teeth! It is not that the dog is aggressive; it is simply that he thinks he can treat people as inferior dogs. Using his teeth, in those circumstances, is, in his eyes, perfectly normal and acceptable.

PROBLEM SOLVING

It is quite common for a puppy to 'nip' in excitement while playing. Try to discourage this immediately, as even a nip from a playful pup can be quite painful, especially to children. Also, small children, due to their size, are much more susceptible to facial injuries, even when the dog intends no real harm.

If your pup becomes overexcited and nips any part of you, scream loudly and turn away, refusing to acknowledge him at all. If you do this each time it occurs, you will soon find that he will lose interest in this habit.

A programme of socialisation is the key to rearing a calm, well-adjusted adult.

When adult dogs bite each other, there is usually very little real damage because they respond to each other's body language and only bite as a last resort. However, whereas a dog is protected by hair and strong skin, human skin is like tissue paper and a dog as large and powerful as a Bullmastiff has only to nip in order to cause considerable damage. So what can we do about it? First of all, we need to understand how the problem develops.

THE ROLE OF PLAY

We all want to play with our dogs and so we should. Play is a good way of letting off steam, forging friendship and enjoying 'quality time'. The way we play is the important factor. Tug-of-war games are tests of strength and, even if we are strong enough to hang on and drag the dog around, we are not showing him we are tougher than he is. Why? Because, invariably, we end the game by letting him keep the toy we have been fighting over. As a result, the dog believes that he is more important than we are.

Play-fighting and rolling around on the floor with the dog are direct challenges, telling the dog he is so important and strong that he may fight us any time he wants to. This kind of play is always employed by the police and other forces to teach dogs to attack!

The first thing to consider is who exactly 'owns' the toys. The 'owner' of the toys is the pack leader. From our point of view, the owner is probably the one who paid out for them at the pet shop! From the dog's viewpoint, however, the owner is the one who gets to have constant access to them whenever he wants to!

Consequently, a dog whose toys are lying around to be picked up and played with whenever he feels like it, is getting a clear message that he is in charge. Even if he does not actually choose to play with them very often, the point is that he has the choice! So, if you collect up the toys, put them away and get his favourite one out several times a day to play for very short periods, stopping before the dog gets fed up, you are reversing

It is important to establish who owns the toys in your home.

41

the roles. You will be in charge, but you and your dog can still have fun. Play when you choose to, and stop when you say so.

A toy can play a large part in training your Bullmastiff, by getting his attention, and being used as a reward. The success of the toy as a training aid depends on the amount of interest the dog has in it, so it is vital that you know how to make him want the toy. You should know which of your dog's toys is his favourite. The best kind of toy is one that he can hold easily, such as a rubber ring or bone, a ball on a rope, a Frisbee or a ragger (a strong knotted rope toy which you can buy from almost any pet shop). Squeaky toys should be avoided as they excite the dog too much and balls can be difficult to handle.

It should also be remembered that balls can be very dangerous. A ball that is small enough to go into your Bullmastiff's mouth will also be small enough to carry on down into his throat. Many dogs have died tragically as a result of this kind of accident. Always buy balls that are too big for your dog to get his jaws around, or try cutting a 12-inch piece of rubber hose off your garden hose and using that!

TAKE IT OR LEAVE IT

Before going any further and discussing how you should play with your dog, you need to know how to teach him when he can have the toy and when he cannot, by teaching him two very simple commands, "Take" and "Leave". This exercise will reinforce your status as pack leader, by the giving and taking of food. It also teaches your Bullmastiff to release an article on command and to take one only when you tell him to. As with all dog training, this exercise should not be attempted if you are tired or irritable. Wait until you are happy and relaxed so that you do not stress your dog. You will need a pile of your dog's favourite tidbits. Sit your dog facing you and sit yourself on a chair facing him.

First, offer your dog a tidbit, saying "Take it" followed by praise, "Good dog". Do this four or five times. Now you need good reflexes! Put a tidbit on your knee, saying "Leave" in a clear, firm voice, and snatching the treat away *before* the dog touches it. The dog may sniff around the floor looking for the tidbit, so wait until he is paying attention again, then repeat the process: put the tidbit down, say "Leave" and snatch it away again. Repeat this stage until the dog stops attempting to get the treat.

As soon as the dog stops trying to get the tidbit, give it to him. This means the dog will be getting tidbit rewards for *not* attempting to grab the food when you have told him to "Leave".

Now you can start to use play to train your dog.

ESTABLISHING HIERARCHY

Bring out the toy and say in an excited voice "Play!" and then proceed to play catch with your family – excluding the dog. Make a lot of excited noises so that the dog really wants to join in. While he is still interested (after only a couple of minutes), say "Stop" and put the toy away. Repeat this

Remember, you are the leader whenever you play with your dog.

several times every day for a few days until the word "Play" becomes a trigger and gets the dog's interest.

Bring out the toy and say "Play". Hold it in your right hand, throw it in the air and catch it yourself. Then throw it for the dog to get and immediately run away so that he follows you. When the dog is close to you, put your hand out to take the toy, saying "Leave". Take the toy and throw it again, run away, and take it from him as before, remembering to say "Leave". Repeat the whole process one more time. By now the dog should be quite excited. Now is the time to stop. *You* are the leader. *You* stop the game. Take the toy, say "Stop!", put the toy away and *completely ignore the dog.*

You can then move on to playing 'piggy-in-the-middle', initially making sure the dog does not get the ball and eventually playing it as a three-way game where the dog is thrown the ball and happily gives it up to be thrown again.

These exercises and games will put you in a strong position at the top of the pack and should be done several times a day. You will be able to use the toy to your advantage during control training exercises or in the show ring. It will also be useful to attract your Bullmastiff's attention away from something that is causing him to ignore you, such as another dog. Pull the toy out of your pocket and say "Play", then praise him and put the toy back into your pocket.

Another good game is 'hide and seek'. Start off using tidbits (or a toy if your dog is not food oriented) and, once the dog understands the game, you can move on to his toys and items of your own, such as gloves, keys and anything else you can hide which you are, at some time, likely to lose!

First of all, ask someone to hold the dog and, while he is watching, put a tidbit somewhere within easy reach of the dog, such as poking out from under the edge of a cushion. Ask your helper to release the dog and, at the same time, in a really excited voice, tell him to "Find it!". Because he saw where you put it, he will, of course, find it and eat it immediately and you must praise him in a really nice voice at the exact moment he picks it up.

Once he has grasped the idea, begin to conceal the tidbits a bit more thoroughly until you can hide them completely while he is out of sight. He will come in and search until he finds them. Once he is proficient, you can begin to hide toys etc., but as soon as he finds them, you should immediately reward him with lots of excited praise and a treat. Eventually, you will be able to ask him to find things you have really lost!

HOME ALONE

The last point I would like to make is that, although you should be removing and controlling the use of all your Bullmastiff's toys, he should still have consideration given to his boredom when you are not there.

When you leave him alone, give him a roast bone or, especially in the case of a youngster, a special teething-toy that will help to remove plaque and will withstand vigorous chewing. Whichever you decide to leave with him, it must be removed as soon as you return.

A dog to be proud of – Bullmastiff 'Alexander' is a registered therapy dog, and his calm, gentle manners are a credit to his owner, Pamela Jeans-Brown.

5 In The Show Ring

Dog showing can be a pleasure or a pain. Only those with masochistic tendencies and the hide of a rhinoceros should contemplate pursuing this all-consuming hobby with any ambition other than to enjoy a sociable day out. Restricted to this limited level, there is just a chance that you will not encounter the spite, wrath and vitriol that stalks the successful newcomer! Those of us who weather the storm until we become losers and are consequently smiled on again, become dedicated addicts and are hooked for life.

I can think of no better way to spend one's leisure time than to be in the company of others of like mind, attending a dog show – either as an exhibitor or an observer. There is nothing to compare with the chaos in the car park, the jostling at the gate, the banter at the benches, and the excitement of the ring. It is the love of a lifetime, with which nothing can compete.

Try it – but always remember to enjoy it!

RING TRAINING

Having decided to take the plunge, it is important that you learn basic ring procedures, which you will be taught at your local ring training club. Here you will be instructed by experienced judges how to stand your Bullmastiff puppy correctly so that his physical attributes can be assessed, and the pup will get used to having his teeth, eyes and general construction examined.

Following this, you will be asked to move your exhibit first in a triangle and then in a straight line going away from, and returning to, the judge. This allows the judge to assess how your dog is moving when observed from every angle.

After regular attendance at weekly ring training sessions, you should feel confident that your little charge is ready to enter the show ring as soon as he is old enough to be eligible.

UPHOLDING STANDARDS

Although dog showing should be regarded as an entertaining and sociable pastime, it is important that your Bullmastiff is presented to the judge, and to the ring-side spectators, in a manner which will convey the true character and virtues of the breed. Dog shows not only bring the breed into the public eye, they ensure that the standard of the breed is maintained, as only those possessing the requisite qualities will fare well in the ring.

When your Bullmastiff is mature, the show judge will be looking for a powerful, active dog, giving the impression of an overall 'squareness'. The head should have great strength, with a large, square skull and small V-shaped ears, carried forward when alert. Cheeks should be well filled. The muzzle should be black, square, and fairly short, with a pronounced stop. The eyes should be dark (light eyes spoil the expression).

To be successful, you must have a dog that is a good example of the breed, with a sound temperament.

Although a level mouth is preferred, the KC and AKC Breed Standards allow it to be slightly undershot. Most Bullmastiffs have a slightly undershot jaw to some degree. This seems reasonable in view of the fact that neither the Mastiff nor the Bulldog (the 'parents' of the Bullmastiff), are required to have a level bite. It is also thought that the original gamekeeper's dog would have profited from a slightly undershot jaw to enable him to hold, rather than tear, his assailant.

The further specification that the nose should be broad with widely spreading nostrils would be to ensure that the dog could breathe freely without loosening his grip. Although the Bullmastiff is no longer employed in such a capacity, these original features are historically significant and it is important that they should be retained.

The body should be well muscled; the chest broad and deep; the back short and straight, with the tail tapering to the hocks. The second thigh should be well developed to give power when moving; stifles should be well angulated without exaggeration, and the hocks moderately bent. The overall impression should be of a well-balanced, powerful dog, presented in good, hard condition.

RING RAPPORT

Needless to say, the rapport between handler and exhibit is paramount, and the Bullmastiff can sometimes have his own ideas on ring procedure! I had the pleasure of owning one of the most delightful characters that ever graced the breed, whose sole purpose in life – outside of the show ring – was to please me in every way possible. However, the transition in his demeanour from one side of the ring tape to the other was nothing short of awe-inspiring. One minute an alert, impressive contender, the next, a slothful picture of misery, stubbornly refusing to budge an inch until he was safely out of sight from the judge! And, believe me, if a Bullmastiff decides that he does not want to show, there is very little that will persuade him otherwise!

There have been many fairly average Champions made up because of their sheer ring presence, and many better specimens who have failed to make the grade because of their reluctance to show in the ring.

SHOWING IN THE UK

EXEMPTION SHOW

There are several types of dog shows and the most suitable place to start for the novice exhibitor is

The impressive head of a male Bullmastiff.
Photo: Sue Doman.

the Exemption Show. The Exemption Show, although licensed by The Kennel Club, is exempt from most of the rules and regulations which apply to Open and Championship shows. Entries in advance are not required and you may take your puppy along on the day and enter both pedigree and novelty classes for a small fee.

The pedigree classes are not split into breeds but into categories, for example: Any Variety Puppy; Any Variety Sporting; Any Variety Non-Sporting, and Any Variety Open.

The novelty classes are more numerous and usually include classes such as Best Rescue, Dog in Best Condition, Prettiest Bitch, Most Handsome Dog, etc. These shows are purely a fun day out and are quite often incorporated into a fete or another type of show, which is not only an excellent introduction to showing in relaxed surroundings but also acclimatises your puppy to being handled by a cross-section of the public who are enjoying a family day out.

Challenge Certificate winners and Junior Warrant holders may not be entered at Exemption Shows.

OPEN SHOW

The natural progression from the Exemption Show is the Open Show. These are organised by canine societies registered with the Kennel Club and must be entered in advance by a specified closing date. Schedules for these shows are available from the secretaries of the societies and are announced in the canine press.

Open Shows consist generally of anything between 100 and 750 classes which are divided into breeds, thence into Groups or simply Best in Show, which are made up of the Best of Breed winners. The only restriction on Open Show exhibits is that the dog should be a pedigree registered with the Kennel Club.

The winners of each class (if unbeaten in any subsequent class) will be called back to compete against each other and the winning exhibit is then declared Best of Breed. If the show is judged on the Group system, the Best of Breed exhibits from each Group will then compete against each other for Best in Group, with the Group finalists going forward to compete against each other for Best in Show. The Groups now consist of 'Working', 'Pastoral', 'Terrier', 'Utility'. 'Gundog', 'Hound' and 'Toy'.

LIMIT SHOW

An alternative to the Open Show is the Limit Show, which follows the same pattern, but which is limited to those exhibits which have not been awarded a Challenge Certificate.

CHAMPIONSHIP SHOW

Challenge Certificates are only on offer at Championship Shows and it is upon receipt of three Challenge Certificates from three different judges that a dog is awarded the title of Champion. Two Challenge Certificates and two Reserve Challenge Certificates, for dogs and bitches respectively, are awarded in each breed at Championship Shows; the Reserves being awarded in the

Correct proportions viewed in profile.

event of a Challenge Certificate winner being disqualified.

The dog CC winner and bitch CC winner then compete against each other for Best of Breed, the winner of which will represent the breed in the Group ring. All-breed Championship Shows are always split into Groups and are normally held over three days.

SHOWING IN THE USA

Although the thrill of campaigning a dog to the ultimate title of Champion is shared by exhibitors the world over, the journey to reach that goal is governed by differing rules and regulations in various countries.

For example, it is generally accepted that it is easier to obtain a Championship title for dogs in the United States than it is in the United Kingdom, because, while the American Kennel Club only awards Championship points at relatively few selected shows, exhibitors have the opportunity to gain these points at all point shows all year long and at every formal show. Most importantly, although there is an Open class, it is rare to find a Champion being exhibited in this class, as there is a separate class solely for

Time and patience is needed to train a Bullmastiff for the show ring. This six-month-old pup is being shown for the first time.

Champions. To gain, therefore, the equivalent of the UK Challenge Certificate, it is not necessary to compete against those exhibits already holding the title of Champion.

The term "Winners" dog or bitch is used and the points

Competition is intense in the show ring

received by the Winners Dog/Bitch depend on two things. First, the number of dogs actually competed against in the classes, and second, the geographical location of the show. The AKC determines how many points are awarded for each breed, based on their Schedule of Points for each state, etc. There are 12 different Divisions. For example, Division 1 covers shows held in New York and the other New England states, while Division 9 applies only to shows held in California.

The point requirements contained in the Schedules of Points are based on the number of each particular breed in competition in that area for the past year, by sex. The Schedules are reviewed annually. To attain the title of Champion, a dog must be awarded at least 15 points under three different judges and, of these three wins, they must receive a minimum of two awards of three, four or five points (referred to as "majors") at two shows under two different judges. The maximum number of points a dog can earn at one show is five.

Unlike the UK – where a dog must be selected as Best Dog or Bitch to receive the CC – in the USA, they merely need to be selected as "Winners Dog" (or bitch) in order to earn points towards their Championship title.

Following the selection of the Winners Dog/Bitch, the Winners go in to compete for Best of Breed against the Champions, plus the winners of any Veterans Classes (usually held as a competition at breed specialty shows). From this, three awards are selected: Best of Breed, Best of Winners (the judge determines which Winner – dog or bitch – they consider as being the better of the two animals), plus Best of Opposite Sex to the Best of Breed winner.

In common with all other countries, the Best of Breed winner then competes in his or her respective Group, and, if victorious, goes on to compete for Best in Show.

JARGON

As the novice exhibitor becomes more experienced with procedures, so will he become familiar with the accepted 'jargon' and abbreviations that he encounters:
Similarly, when breeding is discussed, it is important to note that a puppy is 'by' the Sire, and 'out of' the Dam, for example: "Our Johnny is 'by' Gorgeous George 'out of' Lovely Lily".

The judge will make a thorough examination of each exhibit.

Heaven protect the poor unfortunate who announces his ignorance to the dog show fraternity! These are some of the terms you need to know...
BOB: Best of Breed
BIS: Best in Show
BP: Best Puppy
Tickets or CCs: Challenge Certificates
'Making up' a Champion: Upon receipt of a third Challenge Certificate
'Giving tickets': Awarding Challenge Certificates.

6 *Breeding Bullmastiffs*

Before embarking upon the breeding of Bullmastiffs, serious consideration should be given to whether you:

- Can give the bitch and pups your undivided attention for at least the first four weeks of life (i.e. until the pups are weaned) and are also prepared for the subsequent demands that a litter of boisterous six- to eight-week-old Bullmastiffs makes upon you.
- Can afford the costly vet fees which invariably occur, the equally costly feeding of both mother and offspring, plus the initial outlay of a stud fee and even the registration of a litter, all of which have to be found before there is any sign of a return.
- Are confident that you will be able to find suitable homes for perhaps a litter of ten, and, if not, have the facilities to be able

to run on those which are not immediately placed, while their appetites grow along with their size.
- Are willing to accept responsibility for the puppies should a problem occur at any time in the future.

Breeding Bullmastiffs is not for the fainthearted nor those who seek financial reward, as it can be fraught with hazard. It is essential that the proposed brood bitch is in excellent health, currently inoculated and wormed, not overweight and is at least two years of age.

SELECTING A STUD DOG

Research should be carried out for a suitable stud dog well in advance of the proposed litter. A study of the bitch's pedigree, coupled with an objective assessment of her physical attributes and defects, should be made. Seek advice from your bitch's original breeder or from the secretary of a breed club who should give an unbiased recommendation on available studs.

Visits to shows where a good selection of Bullmastiffs are present are useful to establish whether your bitch is of suitable quality and also to view possible future stud dogs. Go to see the chosen stud dog at home.

Particular attention should be paid to the temperament of both the dog and bitch being bred from. If there is any suspicion of an unreliable temperament towards humans, neither one should be used for breeding. A poor temperament should never be perpetuated. It is not uncommon for a male Bullmastiff to be somewhat assertive with other male dogs, but the degree to

The stud you choose must be an excellent specimen of the breed, as well as being a good match for your bitch.

which he reacts should be taken into consideration if you want trouble-free progeny.

Usually, it is accepted that the bitch is brought to the dog twice to ensure maximum coverage of her fertile period. If the mating is non-productive, it is normally agreed that a repeat mating takes place on her next season without further charge. However, stud terms vary considerably and these should also be clearly agreed between the respective owners prior to mating.

When registering the litter with your national Kennel Club, details of the colour of each Bullmastiff pup are required and it is important that only the colours recognised by the Breed Standard are used: e.g. fawn with black mask, red with black mask, brindle with black mask. (The term 'muzzle' may be substituted instead of 'mask' if you prefer, but the basic colours remain the same). Although there are variations of shade for each coat colour, only the foregoing descriptions are correct.

You will undoubtedly find that most fawn or red puppies are grey when they are born but this quickly clears to reveal the true colour. Brindles often appear completely black when first born but within days, or even hours, the brindle stripes become apparent, although it is impossible to discern the shade of brindle at this stage.

THE MATING

Many breeders like to have a pre-mate test to ascertain the time of the bitch's ovulation. This is a simple blood test which enables your veterinarian to advise you when the bitch should be mated. It is accepted practice that the bitch is taken to the stud dog; therefore, if you have to travel some distance, this procedure saves a great deal of time and wasted effort, as the main reason for a bitch not becoming pregnant is often because she is not ready at the time of mating.

Bitches can vary in their optimum fertile period and even the same bitch can vary on different seasons. It is quite possible for a dog to mate a bitch and have what seems a perfectly satisfactory 'tie', but, if the eggs and the sperm do not meet up, the bitch will not produce.

The first sign of a bitch approaching her season is a swelling of the vulva. Hopefully, she will show plenty of colour

A sound temperament is as important as good conformation in the brood bitch.

(blood) for around nine to ten days, after which it will fade away. This is the time she should be ready to 'stand' for the dog. We are talking about a 'textbook' season here; it is not unknown for a bitch to ovulate as early as seven days or as late as 21 or 22 days into her season or even later. Sometimes a bitch can have a 'dry'

or 'silent' season, which means that she will show no colour at all.

Both the dog and the bitch should wear leather collars so that the handlers can control them without choking them. It is sensible to have the male on a leash during the initial introduction, which should take place in a confined area that has enough, but not too much, room. It is preferable for the Bullmastiff dog and bitch to play naturally together prior to the actual act of mating, but a maiden bitch could be wary of a powerful and extremely excited male and react aggressively through fear.

The owner of the bitch should always stand in front and hold her collar firmly to prevent her from either snapping round at the dog or – following a 'tie' – to stop her flipping over and damaging the dog. A fair amount of lubricating gel should be applied to the bitch to ensure a smooth entry.

There are usually two handlers present for the stud dog: one will often sit on a low stool (a beer crate on its side is a sturdy alternative) to help support the bitch under the weight of a heavy dog. The third person will be in control of the dog; if necessary, guiding him towards the correct position on the bitch. Even with an experienced stud dog, this can take several attempts.

Once he has made a successful entry, the muscles inside the bitch will tighten around the dog's penis, holding him in for the duration of the 'tie'. There is no way that the 'tie' can be regulated by anything other than the bitch

and you must wait for however long this takes. It can last for anything from five minutes to more than an hour. During this time, both the dog and the bitch – after the dog's initial heavy thrusting – will stand quietly, letting nature take its course. Occasionally, the male may wish to turn back to back but, more often than not, he will prefer to drop his front legs over to one side of the bitch so that they are standing shoulder to shoulder.

It is important for the handlers to make sure that both dog and bitch stand as still as possible at this stage. It can be a back-breaking task if you are not prepared in advance, hence the importance of a low seat for the person in charge of the 'rear-ends'. The third person can now take time off to make a cup of tea!

When the pair eventually separate, the male Bullmastiff will still be fully extended, and this is where the flannel with cold antiseptic water should be applied, to both clean the dog and ensure the penis retracts. The bitch should now be safely returned to the car or to her bed if you have used a dog at home. Do not be alarmed at the volume of liquid that comes away from the bitch upon separation; this is merely the fluid which forces the relatively small quantity of precious sperm along the vaginal passage and into the uterus but is otherwise quite superfluous.

It should be mentioned that a successful pregnancy can be achieved without a 'tie'; this is known as a 'slip-mating'. In these cases, it is important that the handlers hold the pair firmly together after penetration for as long as possible to ensure that enough of the male's fluid is released to propel the sperm into position. A tie is undoubtedly preferable, but all is not necessarily lost without one.

WHELPING THE BITCH
Having covered most eccentricities of the actual mating, we now proceed to the gestation period which is normally 63 days. Often, a bitch will produce a few days early or late, but a visit to the vet for a check-up would be prudent if she delays more than a day or two.

A Bullmastiff bitch shows little sign of pregnancy for at least four to five weeks following mating. During this time, however, a close watch should be maintained for signs of any abnormal vaginal discharge. A small amount of creamy discharge is sometimes lost at this time but, if it seems irregular, your vet should be consulted and will generally prescribe a safe antibiotic to prevent more serious infection. It is all too easy for a bitch to pick up an infection through her vulva, which will remain swollen if she is pregnant.

At least two weeks before the litter is due, the bitch should be acquainted with her whelping bed so that she will be comfortable and familiar with her surroundings when the time comes for her to have the pups. A suggested size for the whelping box is 6 ft x 4 ft, although I find the modern resin type measuring 4 ft x 4 ft is sufficiently large and has the advantage of being easier to clean and more hygienic than a wooden one. However, as the surface can be a little slippery, it is important to pack it with newspapers beneath a washable fleecy rug.

Other items for the whelping room are: an overhead infra-red heat lamp; a large cardboard box with a covered hot-water bottle and piece of fleecy rug; plenty of old towels or pieces of towelling; a small pair of sterilised nursing scissors and lengths of strong thread (for cutting and tying the cords if the mother is unable to do it herself); a clock; a set of scales; a notebook and pen (for noting the times of birth and the weight of each puppy); and, of course, an endless supply of newspapers – you can never have enough.

Another sensible accessory – although one hopes it will not be necessary – is a baby's bottle steriliser, plus bottle, teats, and a tub of bitch's milk supplement. We are never without these, in case of emergency. The temperature of the whelping room for a new-born litter should be maintained at a constant 75-80 degrees Fahrenheit (25-28 degrees Centigrade), free from draughts.

THE BIRTH

As the birth of the litter draws near, the bitch will become unsettled, digging up her bed and panting. This process can start 24 or even 48 hours before the whelps appear, but this can vary considerably. I have known a bitch to pant for only an hour before her contractions started.

It is sensible to start checking your bitch's temperature a week before the litter is due. The normal temperature is 101.5 degrees Fahrenheit (38.5 degrees Centigrade) but 24 hours prior to whelping, this will drop by some two degrees or more.

Make sure that your Bullmastiff bitch does not go outside unaccompanied, as she is usually hell-bent on giving birth under a bush or hedge. Make sure that she is confined to her whelping area once the contractions start and do not leave her unattended for a moment. Your vet should be alerted in case his assistance is needed should she lapse into inertia, an all-too-common occurrence in the breed.

Immediately prior to giving birth to the first pup, the bitch will lose a copious amount of dark green fluid. Do not be alarmed by the colour; this is quite normal. Once the first pup is born, you will be able to assess her reaction to motherhood.

Not all Bullmastiff bitches are born to breed, and it is sometimes the most unlikely ones who reject their newborn. Our very first litter was out of a sweet-natured bitch that we were certain would prove to be a veritable Earth Mother. However, after the first 24 hours, she decided to have nothing more to do with the pups so we hand-reared them while she lay contentedly snoring under the heat-lamp! Needless to say, she was not bred again.

Mercifully, such instances are rare and most Bullmastiff bitches take to motherhood pretty well. The main cause for concern is the possibility of a pup being crushed under the weight of his mother. For this reason alone, the bitch should never be left unattended with the litter, as the pups are surprisingly active from day one and could easily crawl unnoticed behind the nursing mother and suffocate. The interval between births should not exceed two hours, and a good deal less if the bitch is contracting without expelling a pup. Should this occur, your vet should be consulted without further delay. He will either make a home visit or ask you to take the bitch to the surgery where he will initially give the bitch a shot of calcium in the hope that it will speed things up; failing this, an injection to hasten the contractions is given.

Often this unexpected activity will bring on the birth of a pup that has been holding up the proceedings, usually on the back seat of the car, so go prepared with the cardboard box, hot-water bottle and a companion willing to supervise a delivery while in transit!

A Bullmastiff bitch with her day-old litter.

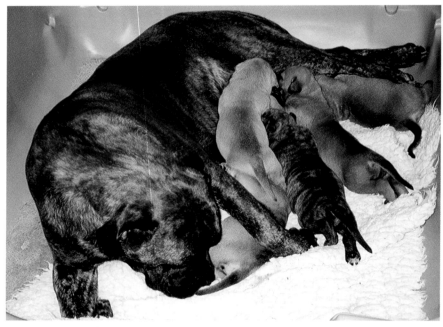

For the first two weeks, the bitch will take complete care of the puppies, feeding them and keeping them clean.

Ideally, a litter of eight pups should be safely delivered within a 12-hour period. The pups can be born in a variety of ways – head first, feet first, breech (which can prove more complicated and may need veterinary assistance), in the sac, out of the sac, still attached to the placenta by the umbilical cord, or unattached.

In a textbook birth, as each sac is expelled, the bitch should tear this with her teeth, releasing the pup and biting through the umbilical cord. Her immediate attention is usually given to cleaning up and disposing of the afterbirth. Meanwhile, you can make sure that the pup's respiratory areas are free from mucus and fluid; give him a brisk rub with a piece of towelling until he protests volubly. Quickly return him to his mother who will continue with his ablutions.

As soon as the bonding process has been established, make sure that the pup fixes on to a teat so that he gets that first essential drop of colostrom which contains all the mother's protective antibodies, guarding against disease until his initial inoculations. Once this has been accomplished, you can turn your attention to removing any soiled newspaper.

It is decidedly easier if two people are present at the birth. One can always be on hand to keep an eye on mother and babies while the other continually cleans up after each whelp. In the event of a maiden bitch being uncertain what to do when the first sac appears, quickly help her by tearing the sac yourself and exposing the pup to her; she should then instinctively start to clean the pup. If she does not bite through the umbilical cord herself, you should sever this by jaggedly cutting it with a pair of sterilised nursing scissors. Make sure that you do not sever the cord closer than a generous six inches from the puppy's navel and tie it with a piece of thread to prevent haemorrhage. Speed and efficiency really are of the essence, as sometimes pups can arrive within minutes of each other and, if you are not organised, in no time at all you cannot see the wood for the trees!

With a first litter, it is natural to feel a good deal of concern prior to the event, but most people find that, once under way, things move so quickly that there is no time for panic. When it seems clear that all the pups have been born, make sure that the whelping area is warm and clean and allow the bitch to rest quietly with her pups suckling. Make a bowl of glucose water available to her and bring her something tempting to eat when she is ready.

As soon as it is convenient, the mother should be taken to the vet to receive a hormone injection which ensures that any debris or unaccounted placentas are expelled.

UTERINE INERTIA
Primary uterine inertia is sometimes experienced by a Bullmastiff bitch carrying either a very small litter or a very large one. Following the drop in temperature prior to whelping when contractions should be imminent, the bitch lapses into inertia, showing no signs of labour at all, although the cervix is open.

The inevitable course of action when this occurs is veterinary surgical intervention. The more common form of inertia is

Periods of activity are interspersed with long periods of rest.

Your vet should be consulted immediately, as this can prove fatal if not dealt with urgently. It is useful to have some liquid calcium on hand which should be given as a temporary measure until a calcium injection has been administered by your vet.

MASTITIS

Mastitis is inflammation of the mammary gland and is most frequently experienced in the pregnant bitch. A careful check should be kept on the bitch's teats while her milk is coming in; any unnaturally hard lumps should be reported to your vet.

Gentle massage to express the milk can sometimes disperse the mass and antibiotics can prevent infection if treated in the early stages. If the milk shows any sign of discoloration or traces of blood, the pups should not be allowed to feed from the mother as the milk could become toxic.

ENDOPARASITES (WORMS)

Almost all puppies are born with roundworms, which have been passed to them from the mother while in the womb. The larvae become active around the 42nd day of gestation and there are safe wormers which can be obtained

secondary inertia, which is generally due to exhaustion following the delivery of several pups. An injection of oxytocin to stimulate contractions quite often proves to be successful but, failing this, Caesarean section is again the only other option.

ECLAMPSIA

Eclampsia is a calcium deficiency which can occur in lactating bitches. The bitch will appear agitated, accompanied by trembling and sometimes unsteadiness on her feet.

from your vet and administered daily from that time to prevent the whelps becoming infected.

Puppies should be wormed initially at three weeks of age and subsequently at fortnightly intervals until ready to go to their new homes. The breeder should provide a worming certificate which states the type of wormer used and the number of treatments already received. At six months of age, the Bullmastiff puppy should be treated by your vet for roundworms and tapeworms, and thereafter at regular intervals throughout his lifetime. Remember that dogs in the US should also be treated for heartworm.

Breeding a litter is hard work – but the rewards are great.

7 *Health Matters*

The major disadvantage for the Bullmastiff owner, in health-related matters, is the breed's stoicism and apparent imperviousness to pain. Only when your dog is really suffering will he show any signs of distress, and this can result in a condition becoming quite serious before any action is taken.

There is really no easy answer to this other than to maintain your own daily inspection of your dog: running your hands over his body when you are stroking him can reveal a swollen gland or an unusual lump; routinely checking your bitch's teats and your dog's testicles – tumours are fairly common in these areas.

Eyes and ears should be clean; most pet shops sell ear-cleansing lotions and antiseptic wipes specifically for this purpose. Daily hygiene can prevent minor ailments becoming a problem.

A thermometer is an essential item for your medicine cabinet – the normal temperature for a dog being 100-101.5 degrees F (37.7-38 degrees C). Any elevation above this is an indication that some form of infection is present and your vet should be consulted.

ANAL GLANDS

The anal glands are located one on each side of the anus. These should empty automatically when your Bullmastiff passes a motion but abnormal secretion can occur which gives rise to a strong unpleasant odour and, if left unattended, can become infected and, in extreme cases, cause an abscess to form.

If you notice your dog dragging his bottom along the ground, you may be deceived into thinking he has worms; in fact, more often than not, it is because his anal glands have become blocked, causing irritation.

Emptying the glands is not a particularly difficult operation – although perhaps unedifying – but most owners arrange for their veterinarian to carry out the task to make sure all of the fluid is eliminated. If constantly afflicted, it may be necessary for your dog to have the glands removed surgically to avoid an uncomfortable recurrence.

BLOAT

Sometimes known as 'twisted gut', gastric dilation/volvulus mostly affects large deep-chested breeds.

The exact cause is open to debate and a great deal of research has been undertaken to try to provide a better understanding of the condition. A popular theory is overeating or drinking followed by exercise.

Preventative measures include feeding two meals a day in order that the stomach does not become overdistended, thereby placing too much strain on the ligaments which support it, which in turn become flexible, allowing the stomach to blow up within the abdominal cavity. Any large amounts of food or liquid ingested at one time by your Bullmastiff could trigger an attack of bloat. Exercise immediately before but more particularly after feeding should be avoided, allowing the food to be properly digested first. This is not necessarily confined to mealtimes.

Although we lost one Bullmastiff bitch eventually with bloat, she survived two previous attacks because we realised what was happening and rushed her to the veterinarian in time. The first indication is a noise similar to clearing the throat, or an abortive attempt at vomiting; very soon after, the stomach starts to distend, causing the animal much distress. Unless treated immediately, it is unlikely that the dog will survive. Upon arrival at the vet's surgery, a saline drip should be inserted at once; this helps to alleviate shock.

If the stomach has rotated, the only answer is emergency corrective surgery, removing the fermented contents of the stomach and then tacking the stomach to the abdominal wall. Once a dog has experienced an attack of bloat, it is almost certain that it will recur and a close watch must be kept thereafter if preventative

measures have not been taken.

A friend from America told me that when her veterinary surgeon operated on an afflicted bitch, he stitched the lining of the stomach into the wound when closing the incision, thus preventing any future risk of rotation.

My first, and most painful, encounter with bloat was almost 30 years ago when I lost a Great Dane through complete ignorance of the condition. It is an experience which has haunted me ever since, and gives rise to the question: why did the breeder not warn me of the high incidence of bloat in Great Danes? I vowed when I started breeding that I would alert prospective puppy owners to any conditions they might encounter, rather than let them sail off in blissful ignorance.

A possible contributory factor relating to my personal experiences is that both dogs were extremely greedy and could perhaps have swallowed air when gulping down their food, although air taken in this way is usually dispelled via the appropriate channels! Contrary to popular belief, all evidence to date reveals that no particular feeding regime makes dogs more or less susceptible to bloat. The fact that large dogs take more time to digest food could result in bacterial fermentation, and the digestion of carbohydrates and protein together might precipitate this.

CANCER
As with many other breeds, cancer is probably the most common cause of death in the Bullmastiff.

This manifests itself in various ways, but it seems that lymphosarcoma and leukaemia are particularly prevalent. Veterinary advice should be sought if lumps or swellings appear in any of the gland areas. These may simply indicate that your dog has contracted an infection, but it is wise to establish an early diagnosis.

A great deal of research is being carried out and, with the assistance of information being volunteered by owners whose dogs have been affected, it is hoped that a breeding programme might one day be developed whereby the condition is at least reduced, although the possibility of it being eradicated completely seems unlikely.

CRUCIATE LIGAMENT
Rupture of the cruciate ligament seems to be an increasingly common occurrence in the Bullmastiff. Quite often, the onset of lameness is sudden, in which case the dog will carry his foot, standing with it off the ground.

Sometimes the lameness is intermittent, gradually worsening until the condition becomes apparent. This can be operated on, but the success of the operation depends very much on the critical aftercare of the patient. Almost total confinement is imperative in the early post-operative period (a large crate is invaluable here) with only trips to the garden for toilet duty allowed, and even those on a lead.

After this prolonged period of rest, limited exercise on a lead may be introduced, with an eventual return to carefully supervised natural exercise. Sometimes the ligament can be damaged without actually rupturing – if this is detected in time, surgery may be avoided. The same procedure should be followed as for post-operative convalescence; there is no quick or easy alternative.

Any dog suffering from this condition should not be allowed to carry any excess weight that could place unnecessary stress upon the weakened area.

DISTICHIASIS

Commonly known as a double row of eyelashes, the extra hairs rub against the cornea causing the eye to run and discharge. If not addressed by the removal of the offending eyelashes, corneal ulceration can occur, which will result in permanent damage. If you have a good eye, a steady hand, and a willing patient, it is possible to pluck these lashes out without having to resort to an anaesthetic. Surgery to remove the roots is commonplace but not always completely successful.

ENTROPION

Entropion is a condition of the eye when a hair-covered eyelid turns in, thus scratching the cornea or conjunctiva. If unattended, this can cause permanent damage and blindness.

It is an extremely painful condition and is easily detected, as the dog will suffer from excessive blinking and an abundantly watering eye. Happily, it can be operated on successfully but, as it is an hereditary condition, it is not recommended that affected stock should reproduce.

EYE INFECTIONS IN NEW-BORN PUPPIES

It is a worrying but not uncommon occurrence that a germ invades the unopened eye of the new-born puppy. To the uninitiated, this is a frightening experience. The young pups can appear perfectly healthy and normal when suddenly the eye area balloons up. This is caused by pus trapped behind the closed lid

and veterinary assistance must be sought immediately to prevent an ulcer forming on the cornea, which could damage the sight permanently. It may be necessary for your vet to make a small incision in the opening to allow the application of antibiotic drops and the release of the discharge. You will find that, once the antibiotics have gained entry, and with the assistance of gentle pressure with a moistened cotton pad to ensure that all of the poison is eliminated, the swelling will deflate quite quickly.

FLEAS

You may encounter small lumps and bumps on the head and body which scab up and bleed before disappearing. Sometimes a tuft of hair will be lost, resulting in a moth-eaten appearance. You will possibly be horrified to hear the vet suggest that your dog could be suffering from a flea allergy. Do not be dismayed; this is very common and the cleanest households cannot prevent fleas occurring occasionally. There are some excellent modern remedies on the market which completely eradicate infestation, with regular application. Do not expect to see fleas hopping about on the dog; it is the tiny eggs that get under the skin which cause the problem.

HIP DYSPLASIA (HD)

Hip Dysplasia is caused by an abnormal looseness in the hip joints, i.e. when the femoral head does not fit firmly into the socket of the acetabulum. Although it is considered an hereditary condition, its seriousness may be aggravated by environmental factors, such as poor nutrition, injury or overexercise when the bones and joints are still developing. It is essential that particular care is taken with the exercise of a young puppy to avoid undue stress upon the joints, resulting in long-term damage.

There are schemes in most countries whereby experts examine X-ray plates of the dog's hip joints that have been taken by the owner's own veterinary surgeon, and score these to a graded scale. The lower the score, the better. In Britain, this scheme is run jointly by the Kennel Club and the British Veterinary Association. If the score is abnormally high, it would naturally be unwise to breed from such stock.

Statistics show that the Bullmastiff falls within some of the highest categories scored. Therefore, one of the most common questions asked by prospective Bullmastiff owners is: "How badly are they affected by hip dysplasia?". This is a difficult question to answer, as even the most experienced breeder – or veterinarian – would find it almost impossible to differentiate between a Bullmastiff with a high hip score and one with a poor score purely from external observation.

With the exception of the occasional extreme case, which generally becomes apparent while still a puppy, it is rare that a Bullmastiff actually 'suffers' from hip dysplasia, although arthritis might be experienced in an affected dog when it reaches old age.

Two theories which might explain the lack of discomfort felt in high-scoring animals are that the pronounced muscle development natural in the hindquarters compensates for any weakness in the hip joints, and that if the degree of flexibility in the hip joint is excessive, the femoral head might rotate without abrasively contacting the socket.

The fact that a number of dogs with high scores have been some of the 'soundest' movers in the show ring and have remained fit and active well into old age might support this speculation.

Overseas, hip scoring is a requirement demanded by most Kennel Clubs before any breeding from registered stock is permitted. It might be prudent to take this into consideration if exporting for the sole purpose of breeding.

HYPERTROPHIC OSTEODYSTROPHY

The symptoms of this condition are similar to panosteitis and young puppies from large and giant breeds are more usually affected. Pain is accompanied by a swelling of the leg joints and a high temperature, rendering the Bullmastiff puppy lethargic and depressed. Lameness recurs intermittently until the puppy reaches maturity.

This is a distressing and painful condition, but should be contained by rest and the administration of analgesics. Great care should be taken in the diagnosis of this condition, whose symptoms closely resemble those of septicaemia.

HYPOTHYROIDISM

Hypothyroidism is a hormone deficiency which can weaken the Bullmastiff's immune system and manifests itself in so many diverse ways that a blood test is imperative

to diagnose the condition accurately.

Typical symptoms are lethargy combined with obesity, hair loss and varying skin conditions, including demodectic mange. In the stud dog, there may be a lack of sex drive and treatment consists of an adequate level of thyroid hormone to correct the deficiency.

MAMMARY TUMOURS

Tumours of the mammary gland are not uncommon and are more likely to appear almost always in the older bitch. Once discovered, prompt surgical removal is recommended to prevent the rapid growth which can occur. However, as they may be benign or malignant, the decision to operate is obviously governed by the age of the bitch. If malignant, it is likely that the tumour may have spread to the chest or lungs and therefore an X-ray is important to establish whether it is worthwhile to embark on a lengthy operation.

MANGE

Mange conjures up images of neglect but it is not uncommon for a dog to pick up one type of this aggravating condition, sarcoptic mange, if exercising in countryside inhabited by foxes. Unfortunately,

the condition is highly contagious and is not quickly cured, the skin and coat taking weeks, or even months, to clear. Your vet will advise you of a suitable shampoo or dip which combats the infestation of the offending mite, but there is no overnight solution.

Demodectic mange is a more serious condition caused by a microscopic mite living in the hair follicles. Although not contagious to other dogs or to humans, the disease can become life-threatening if the afflicted animal's immune system is defective in any way, preventing it from stopping the multiplication of the parasite within the skin. The condition more commonly occurs in puppies and can self-correct at around 12 months of age if the affected area is localised. However, if the condition spreads due to a breakdown in the immune system, euthanasia may be kinder, to prevent prolonged suffering. Symptoms are hair loss, scaling and reddening of the skin. Skin scrapings need to be taken to confirm diagnosis.

The treatment is lengthy and time-consuming, involving the prolonged use of insecticidal dips, with no guarantee of a cure. It is thought that the condition may be hereditary and breeding from affected animals, although they may be cured, is not recommended.

OSTEOCHONDROSIS (OCD)

Osteochondrosis occurs in the giant and heavy breeds and is the result of abnormal cartilage development which causes a weakened area in the joint cartilage. Often this weak area becomes partially detached and forms a flap in the joint space or becomes fully detached and floats around in the joint area.

Although recent research reveals that a growing number of breeds are afflicted by osteochondrosis in the elbow, this condition has been more commonly associated with the shoulder and can be extremely painful, causing lameness. However, with rest and confinement, the majority of animals make a full return to soundness without surgery.

It is most important to maintain a balanced diet with a good-quality dog food for the growing Bullmastiff puppy, as there is every indication that this condition is aggravated by oversupplementation of calcium in the diet which the young puppy cannot expel in the way that a mature dog can.

PANOSTEITIS

Although a fairly common occurrence in Bullmastiffs, little is known about this condition other than that it manifests itself as intermittent lameness which can shift from one limb to another and is often accompanied by a high temperature.

It is more usually encountered in the young dog, hence the lay term 'growing pains' by which it is often known. This is a painful condition that can last for many months but the long-term prognosis is good. Rest and analgesics are normally prescribed to alleviate the discomfort.

PERSISTENT PUPILLARY MEMBRANE (PPM)

Recent research has revealed that this condition has been discovered in the Bullmastiff – a condition hitherto more commonly associated with the Basenji. PPM will be apparent in the young puppy and appears as small white dots on the iris or a 'cobweb' effect. This is due to the membrane behind the eye remaining attached to the retina instead of detaching as the eye develops.

The sight may be impaired, but it will often go undetected as the puppy will automatically adjust to his disability if only one eye is affected. There has been considerable debate as to whether this is inherited. In the UK, the BVA has placed the Bullmastiff on the list of breeds currently under investigation.

PROSTATIC DISEASE

An enlarged prostate gland is experienced by a high percentage of mature male dogs, and is most commonly caused by an excess of the male hormone, testosterone. The pressure from the swelling exerted on the urethra, which is situated below the bladder, can make urination difficult and painful and you may notice your Bullmastiff straining to urinate or defecate.

If the gland becomes inflamed and infected, blood is often passed in the urine indicating a condition called prostatitis. Always ensure that your dog has ample fresh water available to encourage him to drink, as regular flushing out of the bladder prevents bacteria

forming. The most effective cure for prostate problems is either castration or the administration of the female hormone, oestrogen.

PYOMETRA

At some point in their lives, most bitches will experience some form of vaginal infection, since every bitch harbours a certain number of bacteria. Most of these conditions are easily controlled and eradicated by the use of antibiotics. The most virulent of these infections is called pyometra.

Pyometra is a potentially life-threatening infection of the uterus and, if not identified in its early stages, generally results in the removal of the uterus. If the condition is not identified, the womb will become filled with pus and eventually rupture, which is invariably fatal. However, if you take a little care and watch for symptoms, there is no reason why, if diagnosed in the early stages, it should not be controlled by antibiotics, or certainly be operated on successfully, thus allowing your bitch to continue a normal healthy life. The most common period for the infection to occur is within the eight weeks following a season, or mating. I have experienced it as early as five days after a season but the more usual time seems to be around six weeks.

Pyometra can be 'open' or 'closed'; the latter being the most dangerous as there is little warning of the condition until it is too late to effect control with antibiotics.

With an open pyometra you will initially notice your bitch cleaning herself profusely, from which you will see the first signs of a discharge which can be either greeny/brown or tinged with blood. The textbooks say 'foul smelling', but this is not always the case. This is usually accompanied by the bitch drinking considerably more water than usual. At this point, she might not necessarily refuse her food – that is the next stage – but by now it will be apparent that she is unwell and her abdomen may appear swollen. If you have a thermometer and can take her temperature, do so. The normal temperature level is approximately 101.5 degrees F. Once the temperature rises a degree above this, your vet should be consulted.

A closed pyometra is not so easily detected, as the pus will be retained inside the womb, but the subsequent symptoms described above will be the same. In advanced stages, drowsiness and unsteadiness can occur, which is when you have a real emergency on your hands and immediate surgery must be performed.

A bitch of ours with a closed pyometra was saved just in time by emergency surgery after which the veterinarian advised us that, upon removal, the infected womb with its poisonous contents weighed two kilos. It is not unusual for a bitch to lose a cream-coloured discharge following a season, but it sometimes takes a practised eye to distinguish between a normal and abnormal discharge. If you have any doubts at all, consult your vet to put your mind at rest. If an infection is suspected, a swab should be taken and sent for analysis.

At this point your vet will prescribe a broad-spectrum antibiotic as an interim measure, but the result of the laboratory tests will indicate the specific antibiotic to which the infection is sensitive. If the antibiotic has to be changed, you will have saved valuable time by having the swab taken initially. If, after a day or so of a course of antibiotics, you do not feel happy with your bitch's progress, consult your practitioner

again and voice your fears. No-one knows your animal better than you, and if you have a gut feeling that all is not right, follow your own instincts and insist on a further examination.

SKIN AND COAT CONDITIONS

Skin, and subsequently coat, conditions are not uncommon in the breed. The answer to any skin problem is to note the very first onset of symptoms.

During puberty, the Bullmastiff often experiences a condition similar to teenage acne, which appears on the muzzle and chin. These small pink spots are only temporary blemishes which the youngster will soon outgrow, but they usually erupt and bleed before healing, so you can expect a spot or two of blood on the furnishings in the process.

The most distressing example of a skin complaint I experienced was an infant pyoderma which erupted within a week of a litter being born. The first signs were an angry reddening like 'nappy rash' on the puppy's tummy. Later small boil-like spots erupted. If the puppy is only days old, he has very little resistance to fight the pain and distress of such a

condition and can lose the will to live. Dedicated care and nursing are needed, with the administration of antibiotic drops and an electrolyte fluid to prevent dehydration.

See also Fleas, Mange and Wet Eczema.

VAGINAL HYPERPLASIA

During the early part of a bitch's season the vaginal area swells. If an excessive amount of hormone is produced, the area swells disproportionately and the internal tissue protrudes from the vulva. Once the season is over, the swelling usually regresses but it is unlikely that a Bullmastiff bitch afflicted with this condition will be able to mate naturally and she would experience difficulty in whelping, when the hyperplastic tissue can reappear. Although various hormonal treatments have been used to control this condition, their success is not guaranteed. Corrective surgery can be carried out but it is not recommended that a bitch with a history of the condition should be bred from.

WET ECZEMA

In the summer months when heat and insects are in abundance, your Bullmastiff might be afflicted by wet eczema, either through a bite or sting, or simply by developing a 'hot spot' and scratching it. What appears as a small round abrasion can, within hours, develop into a horrifying red, weeping sore patch the size of a dinner plate if not dealt with immediately.

Unfortunately, these 'hot spots' always seem to appear in easily accessible locations: under the collar or around the head and ears – all places your dog can readily scratch. Always keep a bottle of liquid antiseptic solution in the medicine cabinet and liberally douse the affected area with a dilution of this if you notice the smallest sign. Your vet will probably prescribe antibiotics and a cream, but if you are able to contain it at the outset, you may avoid an ugly bare patch that takes a considerable time to disappear.

WORMS

Almost all puppies are born with roundworms which are passed to them in the mother's womb. Roundworms (Toxocara canis) are the most common canine intestinal parasite and are easily controlled by the regular administration of a good-quality wormer. The adult Bullmastiff should receive a wormer which controls both roundworms and tapeworms, the dosage to be advised by your veterinarian. In the US, dogs should also be treated for heartworm.